Twin Flames
Exposed

Why Most of What You Think You Know About Twin Flames Isn't True…and How Understanding the Truth is the Key to Being with Your Twin Flame in this Lifetime

Elle Hari

This book is dedicated to my beloved twin flame.

Table of Contents

"Your task is not to seek for love, but merely to seek and find all the barriers within yourself that you have built against it."

~ Rumi

Introduction

Welcome to the TRUTH.

FACT: Most of what you think you know about Twin Flames isn't true...and merely believing it is keeping you and your twin flame apart.

Seriously. There's so much BS being spewed all over the place about twin flames from numerous self-proclaimed "gurus" that it's no wonder everyone is so confused and misinformed.

And the worst part is that the more you believe and listen to what all of those people out there are saying, the longer it's going to take for you to have a stable physical relationship with your twin flame...if you can even have one at all.

But no worries. This book is going to explain to you why the most common of these myths aren't true and exactly how believing them is keeping you from having the stable, loving physical relationship with your twin flame that you desire.

By the time you're finished reading this book, you'll be able to spot any BS you encounter regarding twin flames - which will set you on the quickest and most miraculous path to physically and lovingly relating with your twin flame in this lifetime.

How do I know all of these things?

I know them because my own twin flame journey consisted of working with some of these so-called "gurus" - until I began working with the world's ONLY truly conscious and successful twin flame facilitator.

I invested years of my life working with her and learning from her every single day, without fail, up until the time when she was no longer physically able to work.

Her awareness of the truth surrounding twin flames was crystal clear, and she used basic truth to facilitate the peaceful relating of twin flames here on earth.

She was the true pioneer of all current understanding of twin flames, but her teachings have been taken out of context and erroneously used in all sorts of ways by many other twin flame "gurus" and spiritual advisors out there.

Everyone's twin flame journey is unique and individual, but when my twin flame suddenly, physically disappeared from my life, I was left shattered on the floor, wanting to die.

I would lay on my floor for 8-10 hours straight every day with a constant, gnawing pain in my gut – crying and begging the universe to let me die.

Not pretty, I know…especially for a single mom with 2 young kids.

I had been through bad break ups before, of course, and even a messy divorce that lasted years...but none of them had left me anywhere near as heartbroken as this.

And I had no idea what was going on. Nothing too terrible had even happened to cause my twin flame to leave me like that. I never felt or acted this way over a break up before...and my twin flame and I had only been together for 6 weeks!

I was ashamed and disgusted with myself for feeling and acting so desperately, and I was completely terrified.

What was happening to me?

I hated my twin flame and wanted to get over him, yet I had an even stronger desire to get back together with him. It was like I was being pulled into two different directions. I was in pain, confused, and I didn't want to live without him.

Finally, after 6 months of this hell and working with 13 different gurus and spiritual advisors, I found my salvation in this amazing woman who was able to help me get over my physical, gut-wrenching pain in less than a week, feel fantastic and happy shortly after that, and even magnetize my twin flame back into my physical world in no time. (After he had told me to "Fuck off" and had blocked me from every aspect of his life).

She literally saved my life.

I continued working with her daily even after my twin flame returned. I learned a great deal from her regarding so many conceivable situations that arise from being with the twin flame in the physical world. She became my mentor.

When she ceased working, twin flames throughout the world had lost the opportunity to work with the best - and only - facilitator capable to help them navigate their way along their twin flame journeys and maintain stable relations with their twin flames in the physical world.

In honor of her and with complete gratitude for all that she's done for me,

I've decided to share what I've learned from her in the hopes of paying it forward...and also so that her life's gift and mission will continue to help other twin flames find peace, happiness and unconditional love here on earth.

To understand the truth is to recognize what isn't the truth, and that includes the numerous limiting beliefs being told and taught regarding twin flames.

The first step to increasing the potentiality of being with your twin flame in the physical world is to empty your cup. Clear your mind of anything and everything you think you know about twin flames and begin with a clean slate.

I know that your mind is probably full of questions and confusion, and you're longing for answers. Believe me, I get it,

But, therein, lies the paradox.

You actually don't have to "know" anything in your mind, and searching for it only succeeds in keeping it further away.

Relating with your twin flame has nothing to do with the mind.

The twin flame journey is a journey of the soul.

The rules that usually govern relationships don't apply to twin flames, and if you try to approach anything with your twin flame from that space, you will only serve to push him/her away in the physical world.

This is because what transpires between twin flames isn't a relationship. It's a reunion of the soul.

Your soul is orchestrating your entire life. It's doing everything. It brings everyone and everything that's in your life into and out of it.

Your soul brought you here to read these words. How these words resonate with you depends upon the current level of consciousness you have.

Every one of us is operating from our own level of consciousness, and we're all exactly where we're supposed to be at any given moment. It's all perfect.

We're also constantly evolving, growing and changing. So, if you read this book once and then come back and read it again in a few days, weeks or months, the same words could take on an entirely different meaning to you.

It's important that you understand this basic truth about yourself because this is the reason for embarking on a twin flame journey in the first place.

A twin flame journey is a journey of the soul. It's about yourself and has nothing to do with the physical form or personality of your twin flame.

I'll say that again...

Your twin flame journey has nothing to do with the physical form or personality of your twin flame.

It only has to do with your self – your soul.

There's a very good chance you don't like reading that, and you're scoffing at those words right now, and that's perfectly ok.

Just be aware that the sooner you accept that truth and can shift your focus from the physical form of your twin flame onto and into yourself, the sooner your twin flame will mirror that and start focusing on you, as well.

But since you've probably already read or heard about twin flames from someone and you've gone in search of answers (and ended up here), you deserve to know why the things you've discovered aren't true...and how believing them is actually keeping you and your twin flame apart.

As you read this book and learn about the most-often encountered limiting beliefs surrounding twin flames (and their truthfulness is dispelled), it's best if you let go of those beliefs forever.

Your mind will want to hold on to them and question what I write because your mind needs to make logical sense of things in order to feel in control.

But, again, this is a journey of your soul...not your mind. And your soul is limitless, therefore, any control your mind thinks it may have, is an illusion.

Your soul is freedom, and every limiting belief your mind subscribes to is a barrier to that freedom. This is why they are called "limiting" beliefs...they limit you.

Our job in this (and every) lifetime is to break through the barriers to our soul...to cut away at our limiting beliefs. And it is on the other side of these that we'll find everything we could ever want (including our twin flame).

The trick, after breaking through a belief, is to then get out of your head because your mind will want to create a new belief to take its place.

Don't allow it to do this. You need to be very aware of your mind to prevent it from forming new limiting beliefs.

How do you do this? By staying present.

If you feel depressed/ashamed/guilty or even nostalgic in a good way about circumstances with your twin flame, then you are focused on the past.

If you feel anxious/nervous/stressed out or have any expectations (good or bad) about circumstances with your twin flame, then you are focused on the future.

In either case, that means you're not present. When you're present you're out of your head, and you feel peaceful, content and happy.

And that's what you need to strive for throughout your twin flame journey. You can't be with your twin flame by feeling bad. The only way to be with your twin flame is by getting to the point where you feel so good that it doesn't matter what your twin flame is or isn't doing because you feel amazing on your own.

It's in this moment that you will be with your twin flame.

That's how it happened for me, and that's how it's happened for thousands of other twin flames around the world.

But don't even try faking it. You can't fool your soul or your twin flame. This isn't about "faking it until you make it".

You can't get to this place through your mind or by thinking your way there. You have to get there through your soul – by balancing your energy on the deepest subconscious level.

To do that, you have to rid yourself of your limiting beliefs.

As you read this book, imagine that as each belief is refuted, a chain that's wrapped around you is breaking apart and falling away…unleashing you into infinite freedom (into your soul).

I'd wish you all of the peace, happiness and love in the universe…but it's already yours.

So, instead, I welcome you to the threshold of everything you could ever want. The door is open…and I promise you that once you fully understand what's shared in this book, you will already be more than halfway along the path toward being with your twin flame.

Don't wallow in misery or uncertainty or confine yourself to being in a certain "stage" of your twin flame journey.

YOU, and YOU alone, are in charge of your journey. The longer you wait to own that fact, the longer you're going to feel miserable...and either be physically separated from your twin flame or stay stuck in the same cycle of on again/off again relations.

With every myth and untruthful limitation that's dispelled in this book, you will see how and why your belief in them has been keeping you and your twin flame apart. And how, by choosing to no longer believe them, you'll finally be on the only path to a peaceful and loving physical relationship with your twin flame.

~Elle xx

"Love is composed of a single soul inhabiting two bodies."

~ Aristotle

Limiting Belief #1

"Not everyone (or only certain people) has a twin flame"

To realize how this couldn't possibly be true, one must understand the Divine Truth of Creation.

What follows is my extremely watered-down interpretation of the beautiful explanation put forth by Elizabeth Clare Prophet.

From the main source energy (god/universe/life force/nature, etc.), numerous bodies of light and source energy (ovoids) emerged and from those ovoids, even more emerged.

Although every ovoid descends from the same source, they all have their own unique signature vibration that they share with no other ovoid.

In between incarnations into your physical form here on earth, you are one of these ovoids. That ovoid is your soul.

When you incarnate, however, you must form two halves of yourself – both maintaining your own unique signature vibration but each with a different charge.

Think of it like the polarity of magnets – one half is the negative charge, and the other half is the positive charge.

This other half of yourself – with the exact same signature frequency vibration and opposite charge – is your twin flame.

Why do we do this when we incarnate?

We have to do this to incarnate into the physical/3D plane known as earth because, to exist in this plane, there must be duality.

In other words, in the physical realm, everything has its exact opposite, and this is the only plane where this is so. Such examples include: good/bad, light/dark, up/down, hot/cold and so on.

We're no different. In order to become a part of the physical world, we must have…and be…an opposite.

In order to experience duality, we must be duality.

Incidentally, that's the reason we incarnate in the first place.

So that we (the ovoids that we are in between lifetimes) can evolve and learn as much as we can, and the only way to truly know and experience something is by also experiencing what it's not (its opposite).

Think about it, if there was no "bad", how would we understand and appreciate "good"?

So, to join the world of duality, we must split ourselves in two on the physical plane and actually become duality, ourselves.

This has to happen – no exceptions. So, not only does everyone have a twin flame, no one would be here in the physical world without being one. It just isn't possible.

Think about that for a second. Out of all the beings in the entire cosmos, there's only one out there that shares your exact same soul, who's identical to you at the very essence of who you are.

It's the most sacred bond there is.

And it's YOU.

Your true self (your soul) is also your twin flame's exact same soul. So, who you are, the very essence of you on your deepest subconscious level, is also your twin flame.

This is different from anything having to do with the physical, mental and emotional levels.

As you align with your true self (your soul) on this level, you will also be aligning with your twin flame, and the potentiality increases for you to magnetize your twin flame into your physical world.

And this can happen whether you've already met your twin flame in the physical world or you'd like to meet your twin flame.

And, only one twin flame has to do this – or even know about it.

Remember how I said to think about you and your twin flame like magnets with opposing charges?

Well, just like magnets, those opposite charges will repel each other.

Twin flames are often described as mirrors of each other, and while this is generally true, it's a different kind of mirror than what we're used to seeing ourselves in.

When you look at your reflection in a mirror, and you push your hand out to touch the mirror, your reflection's hand in the mirror will be touching your hand, right?

Now, imagine that when you reached your hand out to touch the mirror, your reflection's hand moved farther away from the mirror as opposed to closer to it.

This is the repelling action of twin flames.

In order for twin flames to relate with each other in the physical (without the energy between them repelling and keeping them apart), those opposing charges of energy must be neutralized (or balanced).

Again, only one twin flame has to do this.

And this only "works" with twin flames…no one else.

Sounds almost too simple to be true, right?

Align with yourself and stay balanced.

It is simple...and VERY powerful.

But it's not easy. It's extremely challenging because you can't do this through the mind or mental concepts or techniques. As a matter of fact, you need to clear all focus off of your twin flame when you do this – at least at first.

In other words, doing this with the sole intention of being with your twin flame will only build up the opposing energy and keep you from balancing it.

How do you balance your energy?

It's part of a process. The process is much like the layers of an onion, and as you go through each layer, you become more aligned with your soul and more balanced.

The first part of the process is fully resonating with what's contained in this book.

"It's like you're my mirror
My mirror staring back at me
I couldn't get any bigger
With anyone else beside of me
And now it's clear as this promise
That we're making two reflections into one
'Cause it's like you're my mirror
My mirror staring back at me, staring back at me."

~ *"Mirrors"*
Justin Timberlake

Limiting Belief #2

"Twin Flames and Soul Mates are different words for the same thing"

Knowing what you now know about the Divine Truth of Creation, do you see how special and sacred the twin flame is?

There is only one twin flame for every person.

Twin flames are literally two halves of the exact same soul.

Again, you only have one twin flame.

You can (and do) have many soul mates, and they can be in many forms – male, female, adult, child, friend, relative, lover, animal, etc.

A soul mate is a being with whom you have a close vibrational match.

Your twin flame is your exact vibrational match. Soul mates are close vibrational matches.

Under the spiritual Law of Attraction (or the Law of Vibrancy), your soul magnetizes similar vibrations into it. And your soul is eternal. It's the one constant throughout all of your lifetimes and incarnations. Because of this, you've probably known your soul mates in all of your lifetimes.

Soul mates often enter our lives for specific reasons or to help us learn certain lessons. Most likely, anyone who you have or had a strong connection/kinship/friendship/relationship with is a soul mate.

Similarly, soul mates can (and often do) leave our lives when the lessons they've been brought in to teach us have been imparted.

Of course it's the same Law of Attraction/Law of Vibrancy which also magnetizes our twin flame into our physical world.

Unlike with a soul mate, however, as long as the energy between the twin flames remains balanced, the twin flame can never leave.

I'm sure that when I mention the Law of Attraction your mind immediately thinks of the movie "The Secret" and creating vision boards, asking the universe for what you want, visualizing yourself with what you want every day and controlling your mindset and emotions by always trying to feel happy, grateful and joyful.

All of that is awesome. Using the Law of Attraction to consciously manifest whatever you want in life is your right as a spiritual being. And it can be very effective.

I'm not knocking it at all because I know that it works...it HAS to work because it's universal law. In fact, it's constantly working whether you're consciously manifesting or not.

However, it's extremely important for you to understand that I'm not talking about manifesting here.

That's NOT what the process is about and to try to consciously manifest your twin flame into your life will backfire big time.

Why is that?

Well, let's see...

1) Manifesting comes from vibration, true, but it's a kind of surface vibration as opposed to what I mean when I refer to your soul vibration.

2) To attain and maintain the optimal vibration to manifest your desires, you have to feel good, and your feelings are created and controlled by your thoughts. Your thoughts come from your mind. The twin flame journey, on

the other hand, is NOT a journey of the mind.

3) The vibration used to manifest can be controlled and raised or lowered based on your feelings and thoughts. Your soul's vibration is constant. It never changes...it IS your soul.

Also, the objective with manifesting is to somehow keep yourself feeling good, and that just isn't the way to discover, understand and love yourself unconditionally. To do that, you must be aware and accept every part of yourself...and, yes, that includes negative and unpleasant feelings. You have to own your feelings and be accountable for them, and you can't do that without allowing yourself to feel them and recognizing your triggers

You're a human being living a life of duality and dealing with other people and situations besides your twin flame...you're supposed to feel bad sometimes. It's ok. In fact, it's more than ok. It's perfection.

4) The entire act of manifestation is based on focusing on that which you want – visualization, vision boards, asking the universe, etc. The twin flame journey is NOT about the form or personality of the twin flame. The more you focus on the twin flame, the more the energy builds up and pushes the twin flame away.

5) In manifesting, it's recommended that you get yourself to a point where you feel and live like you already have what you want. The twin flame journey is NOT about "getting" the twin flame. It's about self discovery and self love.

Besides, you don't have to fool yourself or pretend that you're already with your twin flame…because you are your twin flame! You just need to align with your self and balance your energy.

The only thing you need to do is be in the process and trust that the process is all that's needed.

I hope that drives home the importance of NEVER trying to "get" the physical form of the twin flame into your life. Your focus can not be on the physical form of the twin flame. It must remain within...on the soul of the twin flame...your self.

If you want to manifest certain people into your life, go for it. It can work with anyone else in the world except your twin flame.

"So, I love you because the entire universe conspired to help me find you."

~ *The Alchemist*
Paulo Coelho

Limiting Belief #3

"You will know without a doubt when you meet your twin flame. You will feel a strong, immediate connection/a sense of 'knowing'/like you are 'home'."

I love romance novels, love stories and chick flicks as much as anyone and I'm sorry to burst your bubble, but this "love at first sight" notion simply isn't true for the majority of twin flames when they encounter each other for the first time in a lifetime.

The truth is, there are twin flames who pass each other on the street and have no idea that they're twin flames. There are also twin flames who grew up next door to each other their whole lives and never knew they were twin flames. Some people have been married to their twin flames for decades and have no idea that they're twin flames.

In other words, the majority of twin flames on earth have the same relating experiences with each other as they would with anyone else.

This is because in order to "know" that you've met your twin flame and have that feeling of familiarity and "home", you have to have soul recognition of your twin flame.

Put another way, you need to have enough awareness of yourself (your soul) to recognize yourself in your twin flame's physical form.

This is all on a very deep subconscious level, of course.
Generally, the more conscious you are spiritually, the more in tune and awakened you are to what's happening on a soul level. But this isn't always the case.

Remember, your soul is doing everything. It's running the show, and when you're ready for your twin flame journey, everything will happen in the perfect divine timing and way.

Congratulations are in order, though. I assume if you're reading this that you feel as though you've experienced some soul recognition of your twin flame.

If that's the case, did you know that you're a part of the very first wave of people who have had soul recognition of their twin flame?

That's right...you're a pioneer...a trail blazer.

While every single person who has ever walked this earth in every lifetime had and was a twin flame, people are just recently beginning to have soul recognition of their twin flames on earth.

What's causing us to suddenly have this recognition?

The collective consciousness of all people on earth is increasing and at a much faster pace than ever before. As more people's consciousness increases, it raises the consciousness of the entire world as a whole.

This is yet another example of the Law of Attraction/Law of Vibrancy at work. As more people raise their individual vibrations by becoming more conscious, the vibration of human beings, as a whole, rises as it's attracted to the higher individual vibrations.

Do you remember people thinking that the world was going to end on 12/12/12 because the Mayan Calendar suddenly ended on that day?

The Mayans were an extremely conscious civilization of people – even by today's standards. Many things that they had prophesized had come true, they knew things about science and the universe that were way ahead of the times and every single one of them – their entire civilization – suddenly disappeared without a trace.

This leads many people to believe that they all reached ascension collectively. (More about ascension later).

But the point of all this is that the date 12/12/12 - far off into the future for them – was when the world ceased to exist.

Well, guess what? The world did end on that day...

The world as we knew it.

From that day forward, the world entered what is known as the New Golden Age.

The New Golden Age is said to be a time when humans will transition from being mind/ego driven to soulful. It's a time filled with massive spiritual awakenings and less attachment to limitation and physical and material things.

The New Golden Age is still in its infancy, and it's dawning is already having a significant impact around the world. As an example, look at how many companies are "green" and socially more conscious.

In order to become more spiritually awakened and conscious enough to make this transition, it's necessary for people to truly begin to know, understand and love themselves (their souls).

And that's exactly what the twin flame journey is...an increased awareness of your self on a soul level.

Soul recognition between twin flames is the very first step of that journey, which is why more and more people and at a faster and faster rate are experiencing soul recognition of their twin flames.

The "first wavers" as they're called, have ventured into little known waters, and this is why there is so much erroneous and confusing information surrounding twin flames.

There simply haven't been many people who have experienced soul recognition of their twin flames before now.

What's very common for twin flames who do have soul recognition to experience (after the initial "knowing" and ecstasy they feel when they're with their twin flame), is doubt - once the relating suddenly ends.

If you're questioning an experience that you thought was a twin flame situation, stop right now. The good news is that it doesn't matter.

Why?

Because the twin flame journey is a journey of your soul.

YOUR soul.

If you feel compelled to embark on that journey, then it doesn't matter what name you give it or what you call it.

Boxing something, by naming it, is limitation, anyway.

Set out and continue along your journey into yourself, and you will find everything you seek along the way.

Even if you've never met or don't know if you've met your twin flame in this lifetime, the more aligned with yourself you become, the greater the potentiality that you will magnetize your twin flame into your life.

And doing so is the ONLY way you can have a peaceful, stable physical relationship with your twin flame.

Now, you're probably close to a freak out, "But, Elle, what do you mean by 'potentiality' of me being with my twin flame? I don't want maybes...I want to know that I'm definitely going to be with my twin flame!"

I get it. I was once right where you are saying the same thing. But, here's the deal…

First of all, there are no absolutes when the soul is involved.

Why?

Because absolutes, by definition, have an opposite – something either is or isn't. And that's the definition of duality.

To be with your twin flame, you have to be in the process of aligning with yourself and balancing the opposing energies between you and your twin flame. By doing that, you'll be collapsing the duality between you.

Regarding your twin flame, it no longer serves you to think in absolutes.

Second, from a physical standpoint (and I don't mean to be morbid here), but what if your twin flame dies? It would then be impossible for you to be together in physical form in this lifetime.

And, third, just asking that question is focusing on your twin flame's physical form…and we're not doing that anymore, remember?

Take comfort in knowing that you have the most sacred of forces – your soul - working for you.

Your soul wants you to be with your twin flame. And the thing about Divine Truth and spiritual laws is that they are always true and they can never be broken.

All you need is to believe in the process (of loving your self).

It's worth mentioning here that I realize some of the terminology and words I'm using throughout this book can be confusing and also mean different things than what I'm referring to. (More about words and limitation later).

Just to clarify, for our purposes, the words "aligning", "understanding", "knowing" and "loving" regarding your self or your soul...all refer to the same thing.

Align=understand=know=love.

Self=soul.

"Loving" your self, within the context of your twin flame journey and the process, is understanding, knowing and aligning with your soul. "Loving your self" doesn't refer to pampering yourself physically or splurging on yourself or living healthfully. It has nothing to do with the physical, emotional or mental you. It only has to do with your soul.

And a brief note about some other commonalities associated with twin flames...

While every twin flame journey is unique and individual, there are certain circumstances that tend to occur pretty often where twin flames are concerned.

A frequent one is that there could be physical challenges to overcome (which becomes irrelevant as limitations are released during the twin flame journey). But there could be a rather large age difference, one or both of the twin flames could be married, they could be the same gender when neither twin flame is gay, they could be different races or religions and they could live on opposite ends of the earth.

Another one is that the initial relating time between the twin flames could be fairly short (no longer than 3 months with an average time span of 6 weeks).

They tend to have similar passions and interests.

They could resemble each other in looks – especially around the eyes.

Synchronicities start to occur on a regular basis, the most famous one being seeing the number 1111 but also seeing and hearing your twin flame's name all over the place when you haven't before, seeing cars like theirs, etc.

As fun and enchanting as these things are – this is magic in its purest form, after all – it's imperative that you don't focus on or read too much into them.

Doing so will only serve to take you out of the process and build up your energy that you're trying to neutralize and balance (which you MUST do to be with your twin flame in the physical world).

And, of course, there are no absolutes.

Non-twin flame relationships can have those characteristics, as well. And not every twin flame journey will experience all of those things.

"The best love is the kind that awakens the soul and makes us reach for more, that plants a fire in our hearts and brings peace to our minds."

~ *The Notebook*
Nicholas Sparks

Limiting Belief #4

There are various phases and stages to the twin relationship, including a "runner" and a "chaser"

If there's one misunderstanding and untruth that's tripped people up more than any other, it would be this total nonsense about runners and chasers.

People, listen up…

There is no such thing as a runner or chaser when it comes to twin flames.

I'll say it again…

there is no such thing as a runner or chaser when it comes to twin flames.

Likewise, there are no such things as any other phases or stages that you must complete or go through before you can be with your twin flame here on earth.

I can't even with this one. This is complete and total bullshit.

Please...sit back, relax and breathe a sigh of relief.

You aren't doomed to being labeled as a "chaser" or lingering in various phases or stages for however long and learning whatever lessons you need to learn before you can ever hope to reunite with your twin flame.

These things seem to have been made up by people who had no clue about the Divine Truth of Creation and wanted a way to explain what was happening throughout their own twin flame journeys.

What does the Divine Truth of Creation teach us?

That our opposing charged energies are what repel us and our twin flames.

How is that a runner or chaser?

It's merely opposing energies. (Think of the magnets).

Now, on the surface (on the physical, mental and emotional levels), it may appear as though one twin flame is running away from the other twin flame, and that the other twin flame is chasing the one who seems to be running.

But, remember, we're not concerned with any of that because we're dealing with TWIN FLAMES.

And relating between twin flames has absolutely nothing to do with the mind or what's happening in the physical world.

No matter what your twin flame is doing, thinking or feeling...it's completely irrelevant.

The ONLY thing that you need to concern yourself with is staying and believing in the process, and, therefore, balancing your energy at the deepest subconscious level.

Similarly, there are no phases or stages that must be traversed before you can be with your twin flame.

Every single person's twin flame journey is as unique and individual as they, themselves, are. No two twin flame journeys are alike, so there are no set phases, stages, rules or techniques.

Randomly making up different phases and stages of a twin journey does nothing other than impose limitation onto the journey.

And the whole point of the twin flame journey is to understand and love your self (your soul) unconditionally.

To understand and love yourself without condition, you have to clear all limitation...not impose more. (Limitations are, by definition, conditions).

Compartmentalizing your twin flame journey into exact phases or stages is the same thing as boxing it and, therefore, limiting it.

Anything can happen and anything is possible.

We don't know how or when anything is going to happen, but we do know that your soul is running the show, and your soul is limitless.

Your soul is a unique vibration of source energy, and your soul wants nothing more than to reunite with itself...your other half...your twin flame.

As you align with your soul, your soul can magnetize in everything that matches its vibration.

You can align enough with your soul to magnetize your twin flame into your life in an instant.

YOU'RE in charge. Only you.

YOU determine if and when you align with your self...not some random person who invented the limiting concept of phases and stages.

Your soul is perfect, expansive and all-encompassing. It knows no limitation. It's infinite and eternal with no boundaries or conditions.

While incarnated, we have a mind (ego) that has the desire to "know" and explain things. It makes up explanations for things that don't seem to have any "logical" explanations.

The mind/ego needs to have an explanation for everything because that's how it feels in control. Every explanation is a limitation. In fact, everything conceived of and by the mind is a limitation because the mind can't grasp infiniteness.

Try thinking about infinite vastness without placing a limitation on it.

You can't.

Your mind will think of a word for it or a color or some such thing to label it.

Even words are limitation. For example, the word "infinite" doesn't begin to describe all that "infinite" really is.

The same is true for "love".

Ask people what "love" is, and they could all come up with a different answer. They would all be correct. "Love" would be all of those things and then everything else without condition because love is infinite, eternal and limitless.

The word "love" doesn't do it justice, barely scratches the surface of all that love is and is one word trying to describe something so vast that the mind can't even comprehend.

Do you see how both of those words are limiting?

They're words used to label things that there are simply no words for.

Of course, to communicate through spoken and written language it's necessary to use words for things, but those words are severely limiting.

Every time the mind creates a limitation for something, that limitation creates a blockage between you and your true self (soul) because your soul has no limitation.

As your awareness of these limitations grows and you clear them, you align more with your soul and the potentiality of magnetizing your twin flame into your life increases.

"Fall on me, tell me everything you want me to be
Forever with you
Forever in me
Ever the same

Call on me
I'll be there for you, and you'll be there for me
Forever it's you
Forever in me
Ever the same."

~ Ever the Same
Rob Thomas

Limiting Belief #5

"You (and/or your twin flame) need to heal yourself/clear past life karma/learn certain lessons before you can be together."

Before I began working with my amazing facilitator and started understanding the process that helped me magnetize my twin flame back into my life, I was instructed by various other "gurus" that I had to clear out my and my twin flame's shared emotional pain body, clear negative karma that was somehow jinxing us from numerous past lives and that we both had healing to do and lessons to learn in this lifetime before we could be together.

Achieving any of those things required employing painful techniques, expensive rituals, useless meditations and candle lighting, and an estimated completion time of 9 months to 5 years!

Please, no matter what you do, don't fall for any of this bullshit. NONE of these things are necessary, and they all severely prolong (and actually eliminate) any chance of you being with your twin flame in this lifetime.

Why?

What is the simple thing that increases the potentiality of magnetizing your twin flame into your life?

Aligning with your soul.

How do you do that?

By being and trusting in the process.

Anything else that you may be told needs to be done comes from a place of focusing on "getting" the physical form of the twin flame into your life.

That's not focusing on your self, is it?

Nor is it trusting the process. As a matter of fact, as soon as you focus on the physical form of the twin flame, you're no longer in the process.

That energy that would be directed toward "getting" your twin flame, is the same energy that repels your twin flame if it's not balanced within you.

This is NOT about the form or personality of the twin flame.

This is a journey of your self (soul).

You and your twin flame just so happen to share the same soul, and it is only through your soul that you can magnetize and keep your twin flame's physical form into/in your life.

Remember, this is not a mere physical relationship…it's a reunion of the soul.

To try to be with your twin flame through usual relationship tactics which focus on the other person (like games, flirting, etc.)

or even spiritual tactics (like manifesting, love spells, Voodoo, praying, etc.) will only push your twin flame further away.

Conversely, bringing someone specific forward by balancing your energy only works with your twin flame and no one else.

And, by the way, if you're as distraught as I was when my twin flame disappeared and you want to get over your twin flame like I did, don't even bother trying binding spells or cutting the "cord" between you or any other such detachment method.

None of those things will work, either.

You can't break or cut your connection with your twin flame. It's impossible because that connection is your soul. Your twin flame is your self, and you can't break yourself.

"They slipped briskly into an intimacy from which they never recovered."

~ The Great Gatsby
F. Scott Fitzgerald

Limiting Belief #6

"You and your twin flame are destined to fulfill an earthly mission, create a vortex of healing energy, feel each other's pain, read each others' minds, experience a true Kundalini rising and/or ascend together. You're practically super heroes blessed with a greater number of chakras than normal schmucks, and you will cause the entire world to fall into complete havoc and devastation if you and your twin flame aren't together!"

Quick! Take shelter! Someone isn't with their twin flame, and the world is self-destructing! AAAHHH!!!

Seriously, though?

I mean, talk about "fake news".

I can't even stop laughing. I'm not laughing at you, though.

I'm laughing at myself because I used to whole-heartedly believe this crap.

Not only was I completely shattered by the abrupt departure of the other half of my soul from my life when our energy repelled us from each other, but I had the weight of the world – the entire universe – on my shoulders, as well.

Literally…or so I thought.

Not only had I failed myself and my twin flame by not being able to hang onto yet another man…but I had single-handedly somehow placed the whole universe in peril.

Everyone within a 1200 mile radius was counting on us to radiate waves of our sacred love over them, saving them from certain demise.

And I blew it.

What kind of twin flame was I?

I was the biggest loser of all twin flames, that's what.

How was I supposed to save the world when I couldn't even save my relationship with my twin flame?

I even remember telling myself that I had to employ my "super powers" and send my twin flame telepathic messages so that he would know that the mission couldn't be aborted...not when so many people were depending on us to heal them.

If you're in this place, please vacate it immediately.

I feel for you and completely understand how much more awful the absence of your twin flame feels with the added weight of the universe on your shoulders.

The good news is that none of this (or anything even slightly related to it) is expected of you or even possible right now.

Here's the deal. Any and all talk of twin flames having a sacred mission to fulfill or any kind of super powers is a reference to the sacred twin flame reunion.

The operative word there is: SACRED.

"But, Elle, you said earlier that twin flames are the most sacred bond and being with your twin flame isn't a relationship but a reunion of the soul. Isn't it always a sacred reunion, then?"

While twin flames are the most sacred bond and their coming together is a reunion of the soul, the SACRED twin flame reunion is what occurs when both twin flames have reached ascension.

To reach ascension here on earth means that both twin flames have to be completely aligned with their soul to the point that the physical world (duality) ceases to exist. It means being fully conscious, awakened and aligned.

Only then, would ascension be possible and the sacred twin flame reunion (and all of the missions, healings, super powers) occur.

And that probably isn't going to happen for any of us in this lifetime.

To put this into perspective, there is no one currently on earth who has attained ascension.

A few living people have come close, and with the Dawning of the New Golden Age, more and more are getting closer (which is also why more twin flames are having soul recognition of each other).

Some people believe that certain people have attained ascension throughout history. These people are known as the Ascended Masters and include such esteemed names as Buddha, Jesus, Mohammad, Archangel Michael, St. Germain, Confuscius and dozens more (including the Mayans whom we discussed earlier).

I really don't know much about this school of thought, to be honest, but suffice to say that, unless you're on the same level of consciousness those guys were on, I think it's safe to assume that ascension isn't exactly in the cards for you this time around.

So, there's the sacred twin flame reunion and what we're doing here – making it possible for you and your twin flame to relate with each other in the physical without all the back and forth, push/pull and highs and lows.

Yes, when the sacred twin flame reunion occurs, your twin flame love will pour out and envelop the world in healing energy and light. You and your twin flame will experience true unconditional love and kundalini rising sex at all times.

You will be aware of your mission and complete it with perfection.

But, first, we want you to be with your twin flame in this lifetime, right?

Baby steps.

A note about telepathy and mind blowing sex between you and your twin flame...

There are certainly many twin flames who can communicate telepathically with each other, just like there are numerous non-twin flames in the world who can do so. But there are many who can't. And that's perfectly fine.

The same can not be said about the sex. Make no mistake. The best sex is indeed with your twin flame.

Period.

"It's like, in that moment, the whole universe existed just to bring us together."

~ Jonathan Trager
Serendipity

Limiting Belief #7

"You aren't whole or complete and a part of you is missing if you aren't with your twin flame."

The above statement is false because:

A. Your twin flame is you.
B. You and your twin flame are always connected through your soul.
C. You are completely whole and your twin flame is completely whole, you're just different polarities.
D. Believing this is focusing on the physical form of the twin flame and duality.
E. All of the above.

Answer: E

First of all, you are ALWAYS with your twin flame because your twin flame is you. The more you align with YOU, the more you align with your twin flame.

You'll notice as you remain in the process and align with your self that synchronicities start happening more and more.

You'll also notice that your life and that of your twin flame parallel each other. Even when you're apart, you may be going through rough times at the same time or you may have a strong premonition or dream about something going on in your twin flame's life, and you come to find out that the very thing did, in fact, happen.

It really is magical and just when you think you've seen everything…you're completely surprised again and again.

"If you find me not within you, you will never find me. For I have been with you from the beginning of me."

~ Rumi

The Process

The name of this section says it all.

Now that you have recognized, cut through and eliminated all of those limiting beliefs about twin flames, you can get out of your head.

You're now aware that the twin flame journey is a journey of the soul...not the mind.

And the soul is limitless, infinite and eternal. It can't be boxed into categories, and there's no one-size-fits-all description about the twin flame journey because every twin flame journey is unique and individual.

The one thing they all have in common is that they are a journey of the self.

To understand, know and love your self is to understand, know and love your twin flame.

How you do that is by balancing the opposite energies that exist within you and your twin flame and that gets done by being in the process.

But, now that you know all of this, forget about it.

Seriously.

This isn't about what you know in your mind. Get out of your mind.

Remain present, and just "be" in the now.

Remember that your soul is doing everything, and your soul is magnetizing everything and everyone into your life that matches the vibration of the current level of your alignment with your soul.

The more you align with the vibration of your soul, the more you will magnetize things and people into your life that more closely match your true vibration.

Your twin flame is your exact vibrational match, but you don't have to be in exact alignment with your soul to magnetize your twin flame into your physical world.

As we've seen, if you were in exact alignment with your soul, you would have reached ascension. (As we've also seen, not happening yet).

Align closer with your true vibration by being in the process and balancing your energy, and that's where you'll find your twin flame.

Maintain that balance, and your twin flame can never leave your side.

Dear Gorgeous Reader,

Thank you for taking the time to read this book.

I hope it helped provide you with some clarity about the miraculous yet challenging journey of self-discovery you're currently taking.

If you feel that you didn't quite resonate with some of the things discussed in this book or that they were over your head, that's perfect. You're right where you're meant to be.

Wait a few days, and read it again.

You'll be surprised at how much more you'll resonate with. Continue to re-read this periodically, and you'll notice that the same words have new and deeper meanings for you. Proof that we're constantly evolving.

The awareness received from what's contained in this book is only meant to clear out the entrance to the path that leads to your soul – and, therefore, your twin flame. My follow up book, The Process, (available June 2017) will actually help guide you down that path, and that's where the fun and magic happen.

I know from experience that this journey requires a guide to help lead the way.

If you don't want to wait until The Process becomes available, and you would like help going deeper into the process, balancing your energy and aligning with yourself enough to magnetize and keep your twin flame in your physical life, I'm available for a very limited number of one-on-one Twin Flame Alchemy Sessions.

If interested, please send an email to:

ellehari1111@gmail.com

Also, please consider joining my free, brand new Facebook Group (called Be With Your Twin Flame).

http://www.facebook.com/groups/bewithyourtwinflame

Here, you'll not only find a safe space to get support from me, personally, and other people on their twin flame journeys…but you will be the first to know of the latest resources that are currently in the works to help you navigate this truly miraculous journey and receive discounts on my books and free giveaways.

I would love to hear any thoughts, opinions or suggestions you may have regarding this book or its content. Any honest, constructive review you could leave on Amazon would be very much appreciated.

Also, please don't hesitate to reach out to me via email or hit me up on Facebook.

With Eternal Love and Gratitude…

~ Elle Hari
Author, Teacher & Twin Flame Facilitator

Ellehari1111@gmail.com